# HERE, I AM

*A Collection of Poetry*

## MARK JOSEPH CZAJA

PublishAmerica
Baltimore

First printing

At the specific preference of the author, PublishAmerica allowed this work to remain exactly as the author intended, verbatim, without editorial input.

ISBN: 1-4137-8187-X
PUBLISHED BY PUBLISHAMERICA, LLLP
www.publishamerica.com
Baltimore

Printed in the United States of America

# *Dedication*

*This book is dedicated to any and all people who have cried alone in the wilderness. Take comfort, have faith, and you shall be heard.*

# Acknowledgments

*Special thanks to Carol S. Luckenbach, a teacher of the English language, for her kindness towards me in my youth, and to the friends who have helped me make this book a reality.*

# THE GIFT

An aged man who owned no name
Left the hovel he called home
And found employment for a day
to buy a loaf of bread.
The boss man paid him with bitter coins,
And strictly shouted no return,
While children cried, and beggars burned
from searing silence on his way.
A tiny man who owned no legs,
Long forgotten in the dregs,
Bowed his head on hands to pray,
yet no name could not listen.
Instead he placed the moldy bread
near the boxes of his bed
and limped away, his work complete,
and cried a daisy from concrete.
No name met his wife wanting,
boiling cold, a barren stove,
and cradled her; his gift he chose,
while love fed her tearing heart
she wept,
and kissed his crippled hands.

# GARDEN OF HELL

I toiled, early on, when it was damp,

and the soil first married the plants.

I danced my thoughts and cared, and weeded

and seeded so something might grow.

No, it would not rain.

Bone dry as buzzard feet

where plant meets the scorching heat

there is death.

Slip away, cursed star, you killed my peppers,

and took away my beans and breath.

Lepers all, the garden fell.

My garden.

My glorious garden of hell.

# THE CRYING OF THE HILLS

In youth your gentle arms cradled me,
and spared my soul beneath your ancient trees.
I walked lightly on you, old friend,
and slept upon your slopes, and prayed,
and found the thing called God.
Then men came with machines while I was sleeping,
and gouged your face, and gloating, laid you flat,
and spit upon your shame.

I heard you weeping, and returned and found your beauty gone,
hauled away in trucks.
Wait, friend, wait, and your larger brothers will fall on them,
and make but dust of their buildings and their bodies,
and piled high, will make you a new face.
The hand that made you will work again, and always will.
Foolish man, do you not know,
He heard the crying of the hills?

# THE SHIVER OF YOUR MIGHT

For barren, dismal months you've reigned,

with fog and snow and bitter gain;

subduing light with your dank night,

while mankind huddled, chilled with spite.

Now daring comes the stronger sun,

and shedding heat, his battle's won;

three seasons rattle to silence war,

you flee far north to fight once more.

You are old and proud, and gray and true;

our Mother Earth's in need of you;

but retreat, in the shiver of your might,

our hope is warmth, is love, is light.

# FLIGHT

I dreamed I saw an angel flying white-winged fast,
bound earthward,
coming to save a lost man's love.
Now raising a sword of fire, bright crimson flames
shot straight forward, searing the indifference
of forgotten words.
into my room of mind these beaming eyes bad my fear
depart, and my heart glowing from a human kiss
begged my tears to fall.
The ice of ages past began to melt,
and my thin soul shivered from hot silence;
sudden freedom.
I floated and flew on wings, above my sin,
my skin flowing and alive,
as death no longer gathered me.
I gazed down in awe at clouds and mist, foaming seas,
black peaks perched along my scheduled course,
and understood the nakedness of all in one bright flash.
I was the I of I on wings, my soul stretching out before
Eternal night.
How holy and free is flight across the worlds of our minds,
how blessed can one kiss be?
Love can but fly on angel's wings,
and tears be but the rivers of God.

# THE LAST SERMON

It went round the town,
In fact, it flew.
People ran, not knowing what to do.
To this day, Mrs. Jones,
tells the story of it all:
about old Pastor Linden,
preaching within those holy walls.
He was standing straight and tall,
reading from The Book,
and Mrs. Jones came in late from the back,
and took a second look.
She gasped and nearly fell face first,
at the horror it installed,
for his top was prim and proper,
but the rest was none at all.
Being the lady that she is, she stumbled,
yet somehow found a seat,
and Linden, he just winked at her,
as if she'd spied a treat.
It seemed his finest hour,
his booming voice, his controlling power.
I too enjoyed it much,

his poise, his praising of the choir.
yet I must admit it had effect,
while we sang the closing hymn,
he strolled from behind the pulpit,
and we caught a sight of sin.
If ever there was truer silence,
I've never heard in life,
Or such drastic pause in song,
or such poetry in strife.
For Linden knew it was his last,
And his face showed no disgrace.
He had tried for forty years,
to get a rise from that stale place.
And me, I thought it was wise,
to help him if I could,
so I stood and yelled Amen!
It did him rather good.
But God knows the wheat from the chaff,
and I couldn't help but laugh,
when Linden turned to go,
and an old farmer exclaimed,
"At last your better half!"

## WHEN I WAS YOU

A child inside cries out,
begging to be loved,
needing confusion.
Time dies when the man of my soul
takes his sword,
faces the pain,
cools at hot summer sun,
swims in creation.

You smile,
and I go back a long time,
to dreams,
to hell a long way in,
and see what I am.

I am you,
talking to myself,
loving and hating.
I hear a baby cry,
wounded to heal,
to adapt,
to survive.

It was true,
when I was you.

# Touching Me Gently

When I stand in the morning
the wind brings me pain
it rushes by
touching me gently
travels on
Though it is from earth
it burdens me

When I work in the day
the sun brings me warmth
sheds its light
touching me gently
travels on
Though it is from the universe
it burdens me

When I sit at night
the rain brings me thought
it drops in rhythms on my roof
travels on
Though it is from heaven
it burdens me

While I am alive
the knowledge of your living
brings me hope
touching me with the wind
the sun
the rain
gently travels on
Though it is only knowledge
it cradles me

# No Dimes

Where have you been?
 I've been through the wars of greatness and smelled
the stench of the battlefield
Watched them as they fell
face first and thinking of their lovers
half way around the world.

I've been through times of hunger
waiting in the street for a little hot broth
Hey mister, do you have a dime?
Saw them as they turned their faces
to the gray brick and prayed to God
Every step means a pain
running up the spine
a shiver
a shake
While one man turns to his wife
 a silly smile lights his face
 Honey, which new car shall we take?
No brother, I have no dimes.

# THE SMALLEST SOUL

The Mightiest river began
a faint tear-drop from God,
and carved vast mountains
into muck on the ocean floor.

The smallest soul began,
sparked by a joyous slap,
and cried to the bountiful
blue evening sky.

Love, more love, and fruits
and all green living things;
infinite bees and flowers –
the fondest of God and dream.

And feeling,
the smallest of the souls' small feeling:

     felt alone.

# FINGERS

still clear water
caressed by pensive winds
lifeless birch
over fortress home

beaver gliding in liquid glass
mosquito drone—
alone with God's hand
as it swirls and seeds
life into desolate land

I am but fingers of the sun
on a blade of growing grass

# BRIGHT SUNDAY

They've recently come from Church;
with city flowers they've dazzled
the drunken early morning Priest.
At least, it is a bright Sunday

in the Spring of forever; they've
washed their sinning clean, and brushed
their dusty trousers free of kneeling.
At least, it is a bright Sunday

as they chatter like sparrows
discovering the housekeeper's generosity;
they've recently come from Church
and they would like a drink

after drinking blood, you know, one
gets thirsty; and one must put
flowers up in a bowl of water so they
might last a week, and wipe the bar

free of ashes. And they've all asked for
matches to light up with. Oh, it's over,
Kid. No need to sacrifice what we are
for some drunken early morning Priest.
We've dazzled 'em though, at least.

19

## LIVING WATER

Placed in a cave,
no water for his thirst,
he sought the things he craved;
a cigarette, some wine, a woman first.
He felt the walls of dragon dark,
feed hungrily on his soul,
and spoke his prayers in silence dimmed,
while waves of death did roll.

Company, a companion, he thought,
would break the longing of the lungs;
though no savior would appear,
on this vain thread he hung.

Through the battle bloomed a truth,
so fragile and so plain,
and finding comfort at its core,
he flung it at the pain.

Then angels sung,
and into heaven he crept.
He remembered at that hour,
even God broke down and wept.

# WILL I KISS HER?

What will I say to my true love,
when she stands there at the door?
What will I say when she realizes
I don't know her anymore?

Will the silence break
like ice with too much weight?
Will I take her hand and play
the happy liar?

Will I kiss her,
though I have no desire?

Yes, I will kiss her,
Men love to play with fire.

# SILENT GRAVES

On Friday night, with their naked faces,
staring into darkness
their thoughts not raveling any farther
than their glasses,
they sit and speak dead sentences,
their eyes something worse than sorrow,
something unspeakable.
Silent graves.

These young ones in blue jeans all come out
to Rover's, Fireside, Café 66, to
drink their bellies full of beer, and
make an art of appearing without hope.

Some fight back, say
liars, cheaters, bastards, and worse
they have a right to live;
their mother is a respectable something, somewhere.

And there she sits.
Her hair needs brushing.
She's blushing.
Pretty if she tried.

Empty graves with one more night.
Oh, let our folly show!

# SITTING IN A COUNTRY BAR

A poor slob,
looking for a little happiness,
maybe the next time she'll dance with me.
Me,
I'll just have another drink,
and listen to the truth.
The juke box speaks it well.

The truth is that girl would dance with anyone.
She enjoys the big-bellied, middle-aged cowboy.
He has a flabby wife at home.

Ah, she's too young for him,
it would never work.
Oh, here's another
with fire in his eyes.

All cowboys please go away,
her blue eyes said to me.
I put a quarter in for a song,
flashed her a smile,
and walked away.

Some poor slob, I thought.

# FRIENDS

Old friends
go on like grandfather clocks.
They marry, they still look good.

We would ride our mini-bikes on Saturday,
drink cola cool and frosty from his mom,
work on rabbit hutches,
eat candy bars.

Playing football in the leaves,
the cold autumn air like spearmint to the lungs.
Go out for the bomb, fake left and right.
What a play!
If I dropped it I was a goat.
Thank you, Lord,
for all the times I caught.

# THE HUMAN CLOWN

In the morning

    we rise and greet the day.

We stay till the work be done

    then return

as if the battle's won.

We kid ourselves

    the human clown

Smiling while

    in the world we drown.

## CATHY

What sweet spirit her eyes shed
sitting and laughing while the world
wed her thought to mine.
Time enough to drink a little;
a laughter so pure snow
would be ashamed.
Her words speak to someone
I haven't been.
Her hair a mystery of a thousand years.
A good wind melts her kiss into mine.

Crazy life, why now, in this place?
See the poet and the lady dance.
A billion dreams might pass,
yet this moment fills me;
I know her.
She is.

# ONLY RINSE YOUR MIND

Only rinse your mind;
and glance at the jeans crumpled on the floor,
and remember the passion picture loaned to your heart.

Look into her water eyes and cry a little.
You might cry a little on your Book, or on
the pillow form you think is soft.

You might wander nights in shallow daze,
figuring,
counting the seasons.

Sad friend, it will not end;
the glare of morning sun
draws a cover over your helpless eyes.

You lie alone;
lover of reason.

## Sunday Night Uptights

Five stinking nights a week I dread
the foggy abyss of night.
The day is dead.
Ah, when the spike has bled you,
laboring man — keep working.
Make the bread.
Drink sour coffee.
Work, work, and work some more,
and you'll be free, you'll see.
There's no better feeling
than reeling in the line.
Knowing
you're the hook,
you're the bait,
and at seventy the current is too strong,
and the angler Fate.

# JUZ A WORKIN' MAN

Juz a workin' man
getting' by on silent wit
forced to eat the food of workin' men
and listen to their shit

At noon I has a special grace
in perceiving minds
and longs like any man
for dat old quittin' time

After works I has my beer
and friendly sneers
knowin' I be back on dat job t'morrow
and knowin' dat 'dis simple smirk
ain't nuttin' but dumb work sorrow

## ANSWERS

One man loved the soul in you
while it crossed the sea of truth,
to gain passage through those waves,
cresting, falling icy cold.
That mean clean mistress knows
a man so young and old from changing souls;
knows good men dying.
No one told her life is crying,
save the stormy sea Reality.

Answers men will always have,
so do children playing.
Answers to the sea and graying
aren't scattered here and there—
like those who've lived and bled.
They are overwhelming,
and lie buried with the dead.

# DAMN POETS

Poets are lonely;
to be otherwise would be madness.
In despairing moments come greatness,
empathy, love and forgiveness.
All have loved something;
some sunray or bright moon sometime,
and having their feet set in words,
they become ageless.

Wiser than a farmer,
more powerful than a child's piercing cry,
they write, and save a teardrop for an angel's
hope: they scribble, their hands freezing,
think a page, and so become companions.

Someone bless them,
with pen flowing and mind going,
going away, going away,
to innocence.
Bless, oh someone bless,
the release of a heart to mine.

# APPLE BLOSSOMS

let me smell the apple blossoms,
release me from this winter, myself.
let me carry a newborn lamb;
find me a pasture that I may rest.

let me drink from a cool stream,
cradle me and give kisses please.
help make the sun come up;
sing with me as I water the garden.

rejoice as the children cuddle lions,
and count the faces in the clouds.
let us go sprinkle pollen on the flowers;
let us tickle the toes of the maple tree.

there is nothing to fear now;
the bills, the highways, the wars,
the hunger.

the whole damn game nature turned
inside out.
now,
let me smell the apple blossoms.

# BEINGS

these beings are stupid.

they fight one another.

they scheme and plan.

they lie and deceive.

they create little gods.


let reality die of shock.

# MORE THAN ROCK

I come upon a green-glazed gorge,
away is asphalt's voice,
to behold a field yet sadder
than the fruits of human choice.

Sunshine spray stings saline winds;
the surf leaps on the shore.
Bold black rocks, a few
proud pawns still true;
embattled,
silent in their grief.

I'm more than rock, I'm more;
she screams the eternal tune.
Her tears that thick are the waves
that lick the harbor and implore.

Some finer spirit than I, soon
may understand
the burden of her sore.

# CHILD RACE SONG: 1974

all the young children
were gathered to fight.
some wore rags
in the moonlight.
there were blacks on the beaches
whites in the hills
if you listened hard
red men would yell
and the mixed were wondering
if this could be hell.

the damn world was gonna fall down.
dead men scattered around.
hills would be turning
to get at their backs
and the dying were to be
tied up in sacks.

so gather that club
come bring the axe.
we're going to fight
be ourselves
be a fact.

## As He Does

The power in heaven searched for that light,
that single light,
that broken arm of that broken saint,
important in smallness,
in the allness of time.

All the power in hell longed to kill that light,
that single light, oh,
how they did fight to cramp and cage that might
of a soul, too small to matter much,
except to God:

when He did touch the thing and make it sing
praises in the days of darkness, spent
saying nothing, being something, feeling the
greatness of eternity and the subtle lie;

you can be anything if you outlive time,
and die, so that you might live, in peace,
and seek what God can give and God
stepped in and said softly ——

Free him. Let him be. He is human.
Life is mine to take or give.
I love.

As He does.

# EYES

The eyes of the rich be clear,
as the frosty chill of moonlight
on wintry nights.
The poor be on the snow,
on which that light sparkles,
diamonds till the sun dilute
the eggshell
and sting all eyes.

All the eyes of the poor hold
sacred water,
and their cheeks but clouds
from which to fall
heavily to earth.

The eyes of the rich look downward,
and hold no water from above,
for they cannot love,
but objects to amuse us poor,
us fools,
to the rich are tools.

Yet what child dreams to be rich,
yet mild,
to be eyes, rich yet mild
with one light.
The soul to burn despair of Poor,
poor child pronounced by fate;
Dead on Arrival.

The rich go home to grieve.
The poor man stays awhile.

# IF YOU AIN'T GOT

If you ain't got no dreams, then what have you got,
you just got your life, and that ain't so hot.
If you ain't got no woman to call you her man,
then you might as well go home, and cook in a pan.
If you ain't got no money, than what have you got,
just empty pockets, with bills all forgot.
If you ain't got no butts, then what have you got,
a nicotine fit, so just have a shot.
If you ain't got no beer, then what have you got,
drinking that water, your stomach might rot.
If you ain't got no shelter, then what have you got,
the rain's pouring in on your red cross cot.
If you ain't got no matches to light up with,
use the toaster, but that costs a lot.
If you ain't got no song, then what have you got,
you just got silence, like some baby tot.
If you ain't got no friends to help pull you through,
then stand on the highway, and let them kill you.

# LAUGH!

He met her at Fifty-sixth and Vine.
She asked him to come up and drink some wine.
He said I know you must be lonely,
but there's something I have to say:

My leg is gone from a mortar I took in the war,
and my wife left me twenty years ago,
for a clerk in a grocery store.
My children all laugh at me,
they say I'm crazy living here.

She said I know you must be sad,
and that's why this wine will make you glad.
You see my children are gonna' put me in a nursing home,
and the doctor says I'm dying, cancer of the bone.

So they walked up the flight of stairs,
oblivious to the world and all its cares.
They drank their wine, and they spoke their words;
two aged faces in the night.
They looked into each other's eyes,
and both saw light.

He said I know I'm a very old man,
and he held her close.
She said I understand.

Now tell me if it was right or wrong;
they had a night filled with song.
My dear old folks…
let this bitter world laugh,
damn you, world, laugh!

## THE END TABLE

Her pain flows into mine in silence,
thoughts are rushed, patterns grow within,
without form, we spin, we toil, long, long,
long, never knowing anything.

We need Us, the I, we're taught to hush, hush, hush,
don't say those words, never.
I'm not, I am, I care, I want, I must believe.
Anyone is someone laughing, running.
Tickle baby and she cries full of empty.
I can't, I won't, I will this going, going away.
We go away, ramble, run.
Tonka truck, look out!
Above my head, we must, but no.
I have, I've been, she waters, she goes back, sob,
drip.
the fountain on, laugh, run, run, run, breathe, breathe,
breathe deep and drink.
She is spinning I am.
Spider, I trust, we are, we must.
Stay, forget forever.
Climb.

# LIARS OR SAINTS

People who say,

after three days dying young,

how they are hoping for another chance

to demonstrate to the drunks and thieves

that they themselves are not;

are either liars or saints,

or smart enough to enjoy the benefits of both.

# THE OLD FOLKS HOME

Dreams of white light,
stained blue by winter hues.
Cold storybook reflections,
rewarding the whims of self in child's tears,
receding from an aging face, now coming into dreams;
half-life eyes contorting from cooling dignity,
exporting fear to black, by gone years.
I see the old folks home through broken seems of why.
Why dying knows no cry.

# No Direction

It knows no direction,
it can take no suck,
lost to the wolves,
it stands shivering above all hope,
sniffing and pawing death.
It knows no direction.

In the baking sun, soaring devils await.
It knows no direction.
Razor teeth tear at its legs,
and rip its blood filled neck.
It knows no direction.

Dragged to the dust, it lies seething,
longing to breathe, knowing it must bleat out
to mother.
Eternal black heat.

# OLD MAN

He was an old man, slumping on the bar.
I bought him a drink.
I couldn't think of anything else to do for him.
There he was, wanting a pack of smokes.
I got them for him and he paid me back.
Preach him a sermon?
Offer some hope?
He was no worse than I was.
Yet I could walk.
He was an old man.
I couldn't help him none.
I felt empty when he started to snore.
I left him there to die.
They say it took ten years.

# A Thing

it is a pleasant thing; living in sleep.
an owl passed by the window where children weep.
knowledge is a door open to a wiser owl than me,
seeing the air pass by,
left here with eternity.

it is a noble thing; wing away in death.
the bird's sad cry only scattered
the owl's stony breast.
seeing was a wise man's woe;
steady as a flickered light
upon a woman's toe.

you see a thing and it will pass;
you know thought, like brass,
grows green with age.

## THE RIGGING

A lullaby sung to morning,
their voices swell.

Mother Earth and Spirit Air,
are bound, blood and flesh.

Moored to this dock, lashing.
Sails strung by force.

Facing darkness, a finite sea,
their voices swell.

# AFTERNOON

It does not sleep, only dozes;
the afternoon my fortress in the orchard.
Time edifying a tortured body of night.

So little is left now breathing inside this hell,
far removed from dancing angels,
well placed in silence, still

visiting prances through the ceiling joists
and window sills;
slapping sleep and memories of her ghost,
warm and real.

## Big Wind

In storms our feathers get wet.
Can't fly.
Boats turn over when the sails aren't lowered.
We live afraid to drown.

Men die, and with them their minds follow.
I'll ride the gale with it clenched in fist.
Men make mistakes, children are forgiven.
Down, down, down.

# A VOICE

No noise was heard in my creation,
save the snoring of my unknowing father,
sometime after the mind of God
thought me to be growing, in spite of man's crime.

Only then resting nine months, to find
I had a voice,
and an inability to outlive time.

# A SERVICE

His eyes shed sacred dew.
His cheeks, carved like waterfalls from nature's grief,
glisten in the morning's newborn sun.
His gnarled, knotty, vice-like hands grip the spade.
His solid foot jams the blade down, down, forever down.

Now the rich, like bold flowers, gather on the mounds.
They glare their patient sympathy
for the one lowered in the ground.
No one liked him anyway, no one in town.

The priest, from habit, had little to say.
The rich turned for home, beguiled.

That ragged man, with that rusty spade, stayed behind,
and wept the whole damn day.

# WHITE LIGHT DANCING

In a shadowed clearing
where the dewdrops softly fall,
there came a white light dancing,
in the forever light of all.

It played upon the grass
and it rolled along the river,
and all the silent lives
knew it as a giver.

The silent lives,
hearing its great hope,
turned away.
Away to daily corpses,
away to hollow thinking,
away to darkness blinding the fruit of the day.

We look away.
It is strangely quiet.

# HANGS HE

Hangs He
of mud and sky as
life leaves love

a mass of bones
to suffer alone
while no bird sings

for the poor tramp
in glory
with young old blood

young old blood
drips to the day
of dust and moans

# MR. WIZARD, 1972

My great Wizard,
I often question your tricks.
With wand flashing purple fire,
little me, Mr. Wizard,
gathered you're a liar.

Saying one thing,
doing the next.
Confusion, Mr. Wizard,
has gotten your neck.

Holding firm as your wand burns out.

Confusion,
being contagious,
I will stomp you out.
Yes, little me, Mr. Wizard.
Go away, take your wand.

I'm a frog in a brackish pond.
Mr. Wizard?

## RAINING DRY

All spirit's parents dirty die,
in yesterday's death out in the field
of flower freedom's waning hour,
as nothing to everything, nothing,
as all earth's children all for a night,
wanting day in all of love's blue,
sad call.
Wilting.
The growing carelessness,
of water eye pollen power.
No one, no one gets wet from the nothing shower.

# SOMEWHERE

It may well be late, it is always so.
Long letters are written, notes dropped.
Telephones ring and ring, mothers answer.
Fathers smirk while daughters fondle a mirror.

A fine fine folk guitar plicks and pangles.
A memory too often sweet.
Long harmonica solos play to an empty room.
The incomplete sounds dance on the snow drifts,
and run their path to the awaiting stars.
A silent God winks a loud approval.
A crow picks a pheasant carcass, greedily,
in the middle life of death;
it bravely caws, glances at fate.
Ice cracks, the earth bleeds and sways.
The fire burns and stops.

Somewhere, a lover surely loves.
Somewhere, someone is bought for food,
and innocence dies of lust.

# GET UP

get up
hurry up
sit down
slow down
feel good
work wood
feel bad
be sad
never more
the squawking raven
stores of shoppers
buying baby hoppers
and uppers
downers
in betweeners:
the screamers
silent
the quiet loud
on a cloud
blackened by disease
of every man
woman
child
livin' life
smokin' mild;
fleas on a monkey back
of yeller hopper holes
all livin' in a mole world
of get up
hurry up
and fate.

# ONLY SLEEPING

There is no bird left to sing,
the goose in flight, the silent things
of barren trees and old men snoring
by the firelight; the night of earth
and the ice comes creeping.
I am not dead, I'm only sleeping.

The eyes behold but browns and grays,
and father Sun's on holiday;
the north winds chop our warmth away.
Oh, foolish Spring, stop thy weeping,
I am not dead, I'm only sleeping.

Awake we will some finer day,
to roses, song, and new mown hay;
to light and love and newborns bleating,
the first of fruits and God's completing.
I am not dead, I'm only sleeping.

# BUCK AND HALF NIGHT

Knowing non work, but what the hell?
Who's edgy?
Hard to talk to thinkers, on their haunches,
waiting for Gabriel.

Me?
I go down and have a drink,
and think Aces,
in intervals,
in small green places.
People get deuces,
and bluff their wallet full.

Hollow drinkers in nightly lament;
something spent a splendid nightmare.
Where do the weak at heart die?
At night, by candle light.

## OF ALL SINS

Glass-like glare sparkles,
swirls tiny crescent diamond shaped flakes
on the surface – steel.
Above, the vulture ever searching.
The enemy is hunger weeping
on blood washed brick, whispering,
a sigh of dignity and thirst;
around they are thick, they are thick.

Warring relentless.
Walking ravaged fields,
a sliver of all falls face first,
clutching freedom; breathing yields.
Greed bleeds life, seeds the womb.
We burn.
We of a dying race.
The proud carrying of the head of someone's
Son.

# THE OLD ONES

It never reaches when drinking,
nor touches anywhere when smoking;
when men are moving, smiling, laughing,
working, then going home.
Christ, I have been alone.

# THE OLD DRUNK

Head resting, arms on bar,
nothing loveless life so far.
The songs next door waiting for the morrow;
his lips trembling, dripping sorrow.
Lost it somewhere in dream,
and that itself doesn't make clean
the soul of a man admittedly sick.
Long for the tick,
the crawl,
only to die before God on the wall.

## MAYBE

Maybe we could all get together,
form a union, picket heaven.
We all want in, we want eternal delight.
We demand equal justice.
Why should one poor slob suffer?
Enough is enough,
we'll form a union,
and earn a better wage than hell.

# INSIDE

I lie on a couch:
through the window the trees are bare.
It is cool in a world a world away;
stealing time, smoking,
the day passes.
Inside is what I am;
it says nothing, neither will it laugh.
I have a blanket.
I am warm.

## WINTER'S ARRIVAL

Every year the leaves turn brown;

they fall in spirals on the ground,

snow comes, blankets them.


White, cold, frosty fluff,

crystal diamonds,

powdery stuff.


I'm looking for food to hide,

nuts, crumbs,

while the human cries.

# A SMALL ONE'S FIRST POEM

We have our little houses –
we clothe our children there.
We do our dishes daily –
we scrub our underwear.
We have our jobs to go to,
so that we may buy food,
and heaven would collapse,
if we were ever rude.
We have our little autos –
we ride in every day.
Twice a year, if we're lucky,
we go on holiday.
We have our shoes to walk in,
so that our feet aren't sore –
and once a week on Tuesdays,
we all go to the store.
We have our music too, Lord,
so we can dance and sway –
and TV and beer,
to while the time away.
Yes, we have our rent and bills, Lord,
that are always overdue –
and with all the things we've got, Lord,
we sure are missing You.

# CABINS AND SHADES OF PURPLE

Some flowers grow slow
into Earth
and bloom outward
ever reaching the Sun

the stars feeling melt
from laughter and remembrance

there are no commas in the shades of purple
only forevers of lives having met
the cabins of rhymes
of strawberries and Spring

the things of souls

Cabins paint for us
and shades await hope
Together lives travel
meet
and dance to flowers

flowers of the mind

How kind the thing called God
that has planted us so.

# PROUD CHILD OF RICH BROWN EARTH

I grew in these fields,
and felt the earth beneath my feet.
I fished with Dad, and caught a trout,
then struck out twice and grounded out.
In Church I found love and God,
from leathered farmers, seed and sod.
I saw faces, friends, family,
and on a ridge, learned how to ski.
I learned of men – they died for me,
and of our flag, our dignity.
Yet a lesser man I would've been,
had not one teacher handed pen.
And I'd have never been free,
had she not unchained with care,
the chamber where,
I'd locked my poetry.

# A MAN

The end is the beginning;

the start is the finish.

When you're on the side that's winning

your grin is very grinnish.


The work is just the worker;

the pork is in the pan.

You're just another joker

that calls himself a man.

# THE LONE DUCK

The steel is froze to your hand;
you're in the swamps, drinking Brandy.

Bam, Bam, Bam, they're peeling off.
Your shoulder, black and blue.

Can't you hit something?
I yell and he beams back.

Cracking and reloading, and the silence,
dear God, the silence.

The lone duck comes and arches away.
Take a breath and aim and lead;
an old leathered hand pulls the barrel down.

No, son.
Never shoot the lone duck.
He is the one that belongs to God.

Merry Christmas, Pop.
I said that to a grave.

Far away I hear a fool fire once.

# WINTER'S DEATH

Moon beams on hot ice where my fire burns,
   and turning up, I lie flat.
Merciful stars, in darkness turn also,
   and cry your light to my eyes.
Winds of earth, you may bend the trees,
   yet I am land, and will not die.
The clouds may ride your tempest train,
   an owl shiver at your wrath.
Yet I inside this frame – small me,
   live for light.
Think no ill of me, Father Spirit,
   that I lie upon the snow.
Die winter, for the sun is my star,
   and my lover in need of rain.

# HILLS OF SAND

You sat with me all crimson dressed;
with your desire deep as the harbor of the blind.
The fire of tequila spilled into the small flat
of your mind in flames.
I smoked and drank the light of stars long since dead,
and watched the night wind blow the branches
of your hair; and darned not speak, for fear
of the many boats you'd lashed to my docks.

Then you spoke the words of a poet,
now nothing more than the meal of worms,
and a voice of a world away smiled
through your ivoried teeth.

"No man is an Island" punched my muddled brain.
I fought its pain and a distant wave named truth
broke and deafened me.

All men are islands, and hear the rising of the sea.

# I KNOW WHY

What's this face so sad and blue?

Yesterday, it wasn't you.

What's these curses and all the fuss?

Yesterday, you blessed all of us.

Why the anger and the pain?

Yesterday, you sang and sang.

I know why you're sad and fumin',

you're twice a saint, but first a human.

# BREATHLESS FISH

I clasped rats in my flat, and am friends with truth,
who lies in a can near the end of an alley.
I brought a blanket once, which sold for half a bottle
from a bag lady; her leprous hands gave thanks.

I saw this through stained glass, and the trash man came,
and spit, and took away her home.
I cut my eyes on a breathless fish;
it bled red streaks on my telephone.

I cursed cruel life while the rain came down,
and then I thought of you; speckless, bright, bold.
You spun your purity into mud.
Your cozy home a web indifferent.
Your soul the promise of a page.

You kept me in a paper box,
yet wore me once a week to Church,
like truth she smiles, and he coughs his last.
The bottle broke.
The county came with a blanket;
you awoke.

Kiss your perfect self good-night, breathless fish.
I find the lesser greater company.

# A SYMPHONY OF VINES

The rain fell soft upon the greenness,
in rhythms;
a strand of muted drums.

I wandered to a gentle time…
the cherub face of Grandma
kissed my childish cheek.

I looked into the well of blues
that painted her eyes, and sighed,
and asked if we could pick grapes.

Awake, I rise, and nearing the hedgerow
where a lifetime ago we stood,
I hear the symphony of vines.

Yes, Grandma, I hear the song.
My children hear it, too.
It is true;
no one ever dies.

# THE ONLY SIN OF CHESTER JONES

Chester Jones practiced once a week,
and would mouth a prayer and smile.
He'd pat a child on the head,
and helped a widowed woman,
who owned a withered leg.

He saved a bird with a broken beak,
and fed it with a dropper seven years.
He'd toss a coin to the lonely and the lost,
he joined the Elks,
and wrote off the cost.

He had sorrow for the meek,
and lived a quiet life on a noisy street,
and most thought well of him.
He died one wintry night when Jesus said;
"My death remains thy only sin".

Chester begged and pleaded,
yet could not enter in;
his soul fried like shrimp at Manny's Place,
and came face to face in that grim space,
with one who's named Good Boss.

Tears, tears, for such right men,
who believed their souls were fine.
Remorse, I say, for the righteous blind,
deceived by that sweet song.
Pity, for the likes of Chester Jones,
who can never do no wrong.

## YES, I AM HERE: 1974

I wonder what to say
    to her
When she looks at me
    waiting
for me to speak

Though I'm not afraid
    of her
when she asks me
what I'm made of

Just silly putty
and a few beers
I think I feel that way

It's a friendship
    I guess
    with her
without having to speak
    dumb human
    words

# DARLING, I'LL GO WITH YOU

Darling, I tried my best,
to make a home for you.
I tried to raise our children right,
I tried to get us through.
I know our house, it ain't so grand,
and our clothes are rather plain,
and I sure ain't no movie star,
but I love you just the same.
We've always stuck together,
when the money wasn't there,
and I'd work a little harder,
because I know you cared.
Now they say you're gonna pass,
onto heaven, of that I'm sure,
and all I can do is hold you,
and feel your heart so pure.
But there's something you must know,
now don't go looking blue,
when the angels come to take you home,
darling, I'll go with you.
I'll go with you to the highest star,
to our eternal home,
we'll never lack for nothing,
we'll never be alone.
When the angels come to take you home,
darling, I'll go with you.

# LONG-HAIRED TEARS

When you were flippin', flyin' fast,
with Cream on the radio,
did you think it would last, did you know your foe?
Or did they just pass, like flash,
when they all had to go?
You fought like a saint, that good fight of faith;
but the times were all wrong, and you didn't belong,
with men quoting Jesus and Poe.
So you tried to find love, and looking above,
you shouted a song of yourself,
but heaven was deaf and all that was left,
was the future you stored on a shelf.
Now you sit and you stare at the places you'd dare
to travel when you were so young;
hoping to care, if you found here there,
with the litter of songs that you sung.
Go on, tip it, and drink your belly full,
and cry as if you've found the places of heart,
that tear you apart, and fester the pride in a bull.
Go on, don't look back.
So what if you crack?
No one is crying for you.
In it all you can wallow,
a hard pill to swallow;
knowing your life was once true.
You're not the first or the last, that's caught in the past,
singing a meaningless song.
But don't come to me, pleading for sympathy,
because your long hair is gone!

# FAITHFUL MUTT

Everywhere I went that day,
people wore a frown.
I could not find a smiling face,
in this entire town.

At first it didn't bother me;
I tried my best to grin.
But the more I went about my work;
the more forlorn and grim.

I went on through the day,
and all that night I tossed.
I could not help but wonder,
if all were really lost.

Morning came, and I walked our dog;
her laughing face was true.
Her tail was wagging and her gait was fast;
the skies were bright and blue.

Never mind the humankind,
who often sour soon;
they rarely seem content,
and speak of doom and gloom.

I often am no better,
but I never will despise;
the friendship of a faithful mutt...
the love in my dog's eyes.

## WHAT BELONGS TO MAN

Oh women, you can have the paychecks,

though they be far and few,

and we'll help with the children,

when the day is through.

We'll even fold the laundry,

and do a dish or two,

cook what we can for supper,

to be a help to you.

And you may have this world,

to save it, if you can,

but there's one thing you'll never have,

and that's the couch,

for that belongs to man!

# ARROWS

We can watch them now on CNN,
and speak politely now and then,
about Them, at dinner.
Skeletal faces too dry to cry, oh me, oh my,
we say, and stuff away.
Our bloated bellies grow an inch a day FROM food,
not for want.
We turn away,
and forget that this world only remembers winners.

Let's all clap for the bomb builders:
the baby blasters that keep our pensions strong.
Don't forget to shake your head once a week,
for the starving meek;
it is never US that's wrong.

We are a world filled with sons of bitches.
Arrows, I say, arrows to the riches.

# I'D SEEN THE BLOOD ON CHRISTMAS DAY

The old man slept on a subway grate,
his days were short, his hour late.
I'd shared a bottle of three dollar wine,
to cure his ulcers, to add to mine.
He needed a shave and his stench was such,
that a Christian man would pray for much.
Yet his eyes were bright and his speech was strong,
and I thought the world had judged him wrong.

We spoke as the trains went by.

I was a young man to him, and paid him heed,
as I watched his feet in the frozen street bleed.
I took off my shirt and wrapped his feet,
to stop the blood, his soul to meet.
I left him there in an alley by the way,
perhaps he died, but I was a better man:

I'd seen God's blood on Christmas Day.

# FUNERAL OF MY HEART

Shaper of my dreams,

keen moon eyes in night.

My face a blue-beet from

mention of her name.

I hold my breath,

a drowning man,

fearing the death of it.

I did not resign easily,

but fought with words and heart,

and what was left of dignity.

It died and passed,

as all things must,

dust somewhere on a yellowed page,

and with age did impart

a noteworthy funeral of my heart.

# THE TEST

We are frozen water,

caught in fast time.

We won't melt.

We won't cease

for what we felt was cold

and brutal.

We are fierce fire,

flickering burnt need

with our selfish poker,

turning our greed,

ripping our blood,

and ageless,

slip wayward

into oblivion.

We crest,

we die,

and fail the test.

# So Sorry There, Mr. Heaven

Somewhere, someone silently screamed
  into my infant mind,
  that blasting a frog with a B.B. gun was sin.
The frog croaked and floated belly up
  on blue water:
  food for fish and a terrible waste of legs.
Somewhere, someone silently screamed
  into my adolescent mind,
  that the girl I loved and her breasts were sin.
It did not feel like sin.
  Truly it was no worse than the frog,
  and a better use of life.
But I could not win:
  a sin was a sin was a sin.
Somewhere, someone silently screamed
  into my adult mind,
  that not believing in the greatest frog,
  who bled too and floated in a different pond,
  was a sin.
I had plenty and made a grocery list and He sent
  me to the cleaners.
I'm over the frog. I'm free from the frog:
  send me to hell, if you will,
  I cannot forget the girl.
So sorry there, Mr. Heaven,
  but you have not changed the world.

# FLYING JOHNNY FLYNN

The sun was flowing bright that morn,
and Johnny was runnin' late.
He gulped down but a muffin,
kissed his mom, ran to the gate.
He hopped into his Vette, turned the key,
and cranked it up, and Dad stood there smiling,
when he dumped the clutch and smoked the pups.
Down the drive and driving mean,
a power shift to second, and on to seventeen.
Going slow was just too boring,
and Johnny sure could drive,
he had his Vette at fifty,
the past Allyn Brook, was pushin' sixty-five.
He hammered into fourth gear,
but the sun got in his eyes,
and all he saw was orange.
He blinked and turned to mush-
for he also ate for breakfast,
the bumper of a bus.
Now Johnny's just a floatin',
looking down at all the fuss.
There's no more kissing Betty, no more laughter,
no more rush.
And hardly one week later, in a ceremony grim,
We the People all took it in on the chin,
when thirteen men in suits and ties,
named a speed bump and a stone,
for Flying Johnny Flynn.

# OLD TOM

I'd ride my bike, that's what I liked, when I was young,
and breathing felt good, down to see Old Tom at the dump.
They said he was a fool, and hadn't come from anywhere,
but doing as I should I loved the feller just the same.
I'd come riding up to his shack, and he'd smile and wave and dance,
and I knew he'd be a better man, if given half a chance.
Oh, Sure, he drank a lake, and his beard was long and gray,
and yes, he had a funny smell; no 'tilities, they'd say.
Yet Tom had somethin' for me, a tire, or tube, or traps,
or a piece of oak for my Dad, copper wire or burlap sacks.
They say he married once, to somethin' called a tart,
but Tom didn't talk of it much, but his eyes betrayed his heart.
Turkey mornin' it was, I remember well,
I had a gift for Tom, a fresh pack of Lucky's I stole, do tell!
I came up the road, the dump in sight, the smell was just the same,
and there was no smoke from his stack, it was cold, drizzlin' rain.
I parked my bike, kickin' down the stand,
ran and knocked the door to his shack, and waited for a minute,
but Tom didn't answer back.
I took a breath and opened the door, to find my dear old friend,
and saw he lay upon the floor, asleep, but then I looked again.
His face was grinning, and full of light,
he had the Good Book on his chest,
and when I got closer still I saw his coat,
his mended one, his best.
I went up to him and looking down, saw a page addressed to me,
tucked neatly into God's good book.
I picked it up, I read, I shook.

"Tonight I'm passing on, young friend, don't go crying over me.
I know where I belong. Tomorrow is Thanksgiving day, I'll hear

the heavenly song. Take my book, it's all I've got, and read. As you grow and go through life, it's all you'll ever need."

Well, I guess I stayed too long, cause Dad came calling, and Mom too, came along.
They found me cryin' next to my friend Tom, reading from the Pslams, aloud.

Mom was cryin' too, but Dad looked kinda' proud.
He picked me up and we headed home, Mom was pushin' my bike, and as we walked I kept on thinking, what was heaven like?

"It's pretty there," my Dad said, "like the orchards in the Spring."
And I thought awhile and added in, "That's where the angels sing!"

I'm old now, Doc, so let me die, so take these pumps and pills and things!
I've had a long and goodly life, now please let me rest.
But do me a turn, would you, Doc, and lay that Book upon my chest?
You see, young man, I've got a trump, to think…from old Tom, an old man at a dump.

# WHY I WRITE THESE POEMS

I write these poems
from thoughts in my head,
thoughts, they are hard things,
they can cut you or drive you mad,
they can make you a million,
make you something,
make you a king or just some poor wise pauper,
a clown,
a table or a chair.
Better still they can make you aware,
they tell you that you think,
your mind turns,
you are,
you think you are but who'll ever read them?
Your girlfriend perhaps,
or someone who takes pity and says,
"yeah, that's good, I understand",
even when they really don't,
cause they're not you.
Thoughts, strung together without purpose or place,
just a being, something, caught.
You'll never write the good one, there is always another,
some other poor man suffering,
another tramp on the bottle,
another woman in pain,
another sunset,
someone will write a poem,
someone else will never understand.
I write these poems
to prove
that I'm not dead.

# ON POETS

Poets are lonely.
To be otherwise would be madness.
In their despairing moments come greatness,
come words filled with empathy, love and that
special charity of forgiveness.
Seemingly all have loved something,
some sunray or a bright moon sometime,
and having their feet set in words their language becomes ageless,
and so limitless becomes their souls.
Perhaps wiser than a gray haired farmer,
more powerful than a child's piercing cry,
they, who blessed with infinity, write,
and save a teardrop for an angel's hope.
Oh what dear friends they make,
if having any they suppose in speaking will come closer,
closer than the words they scribble, their hands freezing,
think a page, and so become companions.
Someone bless the old fellow, with pen flowing
and mind going, going away,
back in time to where his innocence captured a rarity,
oh someone bless him who,
when I read,
releases his heart to mine.

# THE RATS OF POVERTY

They gnaw at the corners of my room,
these rats,
that gorge themselves on confidence,
and nest-build on ego.
Fat their jowls become from supping, slurping,
on my self-respect.
Clawing, they wait outside the door of good intent,
forever hungry.
Gloating, they happily live,
to plague my dreams.
Make them sleepy, and beckon them hither,
when the needs arise, so I might survive, and
realize that all of me is a rat myself?
Nay, better to let them eat their fill, for without
these rats, I'd have no room.

# FRIENDS

How often in young life I've sought them,
dancing in the coal of night,
shedding wisdom into the wispy white of clouds,
the shrouds of forests fighting back against their laughter
and goodness bright.

I miss their company when the days hide their faces with a blue shawl,
and their sister sun glows gold and warms the free-loading earth.

Yet my life passes away,
and in my steps they watch from a billion miles,
my works they judge with their truth,
which is light,
and they send their angels near to teach me
that heaven's within my reach,
if I could but doubt no more and
realize they are my friends.

# FIDO FALLS ASLEEP

A fine folk guitar plicks and pangles,
stirring a memory sweet.
A harmonica screams to an empty room:
the incomplete sounds dance on the snow drifts,
and run their care up star beams.
A silent God winks a loud approval.

A crow picks a pheasant carcass, carelessly,
in the middle-life of death.
It caws, glances at fate. Ice cracks, the earth
bleeds and sways. The fire blazes but chokes
for breath.

In gloom, a lover surely loves,
and innocence suckles lust – that
bastard beast of us so clean. Ah,
damnable distant dream, waning, and
you sitting, glowing, a worried dog
chained by knowing.

## COMFORT

Comfort fools itself

with greed and food and rest:

all Kings think their reign is forever.

The slave waits and grows strong,

beatings only serve to strengthen him,

and hunger grows his soul.

Hunger grows his soul until, O blessed justice,

he rises up, empowered, and finds the King

a sorry pig with a title;

and even in his rage,

showered him with pity, not a spear.

Smile, oh blessed poor:

all worlds, all systems fall from this one truth;

those oppressed survive,

while the King but eats himself to death.

# IT'S HARD TO TELL
## (SUNG TO THE TUNE OF "SILVER BELLS")

People pushing, people shoving,
and the Visa card's due.
In the air there's a feeling of Christmas.

People grabbing, fourteen stabbings,
and a case of the flu,
and on every street corner you'll hear.

"It's hard to tell, could this be hell?"
It's Christmastime in the city.
Suffering, while Retail sings.
Soon it will be Christmas Day!

People sneezing, the homeless freezing,
while Mercedes roll by.
In the air there's a feeling of Christmas.

No, that's not hugging, it's just a mugging,
and the hungry still die,
yet you won't hear a soul asking why?

"It's hard to tell, could this be hell?"
It's Christmastime in the city.
The greed of things, but what'd He bring?
Soon it will be Christmas Day.

Printed in the United States
32695LVS00002B/1-51

9 781413 781878